Leadership-Followership
360°

How to Create
Accountable, Flexible, and
Dynamic Teams

JEF WILLIAMS

ISBN: 0615471870
ISBN-13: 9780615471877

Printed in the United States of America

Edited by Jacquie Vick, Words on Paper, LLC

Cover design by Mike Jones, Wisdom Works, Inc.

For information on book and speaking engagements, contact:

Jef Williams
P.O. Box 1132
O'Fallon, IL 62269

www.jefwilliams.com
jef@jefwilliams.com
jcw@jcwteamconsultants.com

Contents

Forward   *v*

Acknowledgments   *vii*

Introduction   *ix*

SECTION A: TAKE A GOOD LOOK AT YOURSELF

Chapter 1   When Self Matters   3

SECTION B: KNOW YOUR ROLES ON THE TEAM

Chapter 2   Leadership   19

Chapter 3   Followership: The Reason for Leadership   33

Chapter 4   Followership Explored   39

Chapter 5   Terminology of Exemplary
             Followership   47

Chapter 6   The Leader-Follower:
             Two Roles in One   55

Chapter 7   The Leader- Follower
             Relationship   63

Chapter 8   Leadership + Followership
             = Results   73

SECTION C: OPERATE AS ONE TEAM

Chapter 9   Many Members Yet One Team   81

Chapter 10   Leadership-Followership:
             Putting It Into Practice   89

Chapter 11   Now What?   95

Forward

Why do geese fly in V formation?

Jeffrey A. Scott (2005) an aerospace engineer specializing in aerodynamic analysis and conceptual design, provides the following:

> Even though the V formation benefits all of the birds, the bird in the lead position has to work the hardest. When this bird tires, it will drop out of the lead position and fall further back into one of the lines of the V. Another bird from further back will rapidly move forward to take the leading position and maintain the formation. The two birds in the furthest trailing positions also tire more rapidly than those in the middle, so these positions are also rotated frequently to spread the most fatiguing locations throughout the flock. This cyclical rearrangement gives all birds the

responsibility of being the leader as well as a chance to enjoy the maximum benefits of being in the middle of the formation. This sense of teamwork comes naturally since even the youngest members of the flock rapidly realize that it takes less work to fly in a V formation than it does to fly alone.

This explanation captures the essence of leadership-followership and how it impacts teamwork. After reading this book, I hope you will be inspired to embrace the importance of dynamic leadership-followership and its place in today's society.

Acknowledgments

I give honor to God and my Lord and Savior Jesus Christ because without them, none of this would be possible. Much love for my dear wife Cynthia, mother Anne and sister Shari for their never-ending support. To my sons Joshua and Jacob, may this book encourage you in your future endeavors. Jacquie Vick, an exceptional editor and tremendous talent, thank you for your patience and expertise. Special thanks to Mark Fields, Willie J. Ferguson, II, Mike Jones, Jose A. Mercado, Nehemiah Johnson, Norris L. Roberts, Jr., Mr. John H. Bonapart, Jr., and Major General Steven Lepper– men whose wisdom and encouragement I value; and many thanks to Pastor Shawn L. Buckhanan, Pastor Martin J. Harris, Min. Sabrina Hill, Debra Dickson, Elder T. Allen Bartee, and Elder Michael E. Miller for your powerful prayers and for always interceding on my behalf.

Introduction

"You cannot be a leader, and ask other people to follow you, unless you know how to follow, too."

Sam Rayburn

What does it take to get people from diverse experiences to enjoy working together toward a common goal? Whether it's on the job, at school, in the home, or even at church, [unhealthy] conflict seems to take center stage. It is an issue that costs companies millions of dollars to address, and has caused relationships to end on a tragic note. During my last few years in the United States Air Force, I was privileged to work in an environment where people were respected for their gifts and talents and not solely on their rank. Leadership had the utmost respect for staff; and staff had the utmost respect for leadership. But I realized I was in a unique situation, based on the horror stories I'd heard regarding office morale in other working environments.

These stories revealed that both the staff and the leaders were unhappy with each other, for varied reasons. Staff members complained about the lack of respect and autonomy, the inability to voice their ideas and concerns, poor leadership, lack of teamwork, and the fear of retribution. Leaders, on the other hand, complained about the lack of respect, lack of initiative, poor followership, incompetence, lack of trust, lack of teamwork, constant complaining without providing solutions, constant bickering, and an unwillingness to go beyond the call of duty on the part of staff members.

It appears that leaders and followers have the same concerns, and I quickly realized that this type of dysfunction does not discriminate and can wreak havoc on an organization. For example, I recall attending a meeting for a volunteer organization where the members were electing new officers. Those who were campaigning for election were trying their best to ensure they won the vote; and after winning the vote, things for the organization went sour because the newly elected officers did nothing to improve the organization. They were content with just having the title of president or vice president on their performance appraisal report or resume. As a result, many of the members decided to leave the organization.

Another situation I witnessed dealt with the ineffectiveness of team members. The leader worked tirelessly to motivate and inspire the group to do some exciting things for the community. To the leader's dismay, several of the members used their efforts to stifle growth and act as a stumbling block for the leader. These individuals were bitter because they were not in charge and wanted to do it their way.

In both examples, poor leadership and poor followership can destroy an organization or a team. One could argue that it's the leader's responsibility to fix the situation in these scenarios. In fact, the burden is often placed upon leadership to motivate and influence people to accomplish the mission. This is unfortunate. To have an effective work environment, things must change. What I believe must occur is a relationship that shares the burden of responsibility. Exemplary leadership is just one aspect of a dynamic team. What about exemplary followership? Followership is a concept that has not reached the same level of fame as leadership. It is an unspoken reality. According to Roger Adair (2003), followership symbolizes a follower who shares in an influence relationship among leaders and other followers with the intent to support leaders who reflect their mutual purposes.

For many years, academia has demonstrated its infatuation with leadership to the point where followership–which is what determines leadership–was rarely mentioned and often times neglected. It wasn't until 1967, that there was even official mention of the importance of followership (Nolan, 2001). There are some who think that followership does not need to be discussed because it's something we all inherently learn to do. However, I would argue that followership is something that must be taught, so that the negative stereotype of the role of follower can diminish.

The discussion on followership must rise to the forefront and share the stage with leadership if organizations are to succeed in their rapid and ever-changing environment. There are two main reasons why followership dialog is a must:

1. It is a function we all perform regardless of duty, title, or position.

2. It is a function that one must perform when serving on a dynamic team that strives to achieve dynamic results.

We can no longer lay the blame squarely on the shoulders of leaders when things go awry. If followers are expected to execute the vision of leaders, they must also understand their role in terms of responsibility and accountability. Once this has been established, the ability to operate as a team becomes possible. Divided into three sections, this book will discuss three key concepts that must take place if an organization or team is to succeed: *Take a Good Look at Yourself, Know Your Role on the Team, and Operate as One Team.* (For easy recall, just think of **TKO)**.

I firmly believe that when a person understands who they are, they will admirably serve in their role as an exemplary leader and/or follower with the goal of operating as a dynamic team that produces dynamic results, such as increased productivity, high morale, and for those in it for the money, increased profits! It is my hope that this book speaks to the heart and helps individuals become the catalyst that brings about great results.

SECTION A:

TAKE A GOOD LOOK AT YOURSELF

Chapter 1: When Self Matters

"The unexamined life is not worth living."

Socrates

"I'm starting with the man in the mirror. I'm asking him to change his ways. And no message could have been any clearer, if you wanna make the world a better place take a look at yourself and then make a change." These words, sung by the late pop star Michael Jackson, drew the attention of millions of listeners and challenged them to look within to make this world a better place. What better place to start than with yourself.

People often look to others to change, and in some cases find it easier to point the finger at another person when there is a problem in a relationship. Yet, it takes more courage to be able to look in the mirror and admit that you are or could be the problem. According to Ira Chaleff (2003), founder and president of Executive Coaching & Consulting Associates and author of *the Courageous Follower,* in order to understand your role in the relationship, it is important to know yourself. Courage in relationships starts with an honest examination of self.

One day I was sitting at home flipping through the television channels and came across the finale of a reality show called "Top Chef." The two finalists, Mike and Carl, had to prepare their best dish to wow a panel of expert judges. As an added twist, they were allowed to choose two of their former competitors who had been eliminated from the competition. Mike was described as a very likeable and talented chef and Carl was described as exceptionally talented, but difficult to get along with. As I watched the show, Mike showed exceptional leadership skills and treated his teammates with respect. Each set aside their role as competitor and put on their teammate hat.

Carl's team was different. He selected a competitor that he frequently clashed with on the set. The other individual was pretty neutral. Things got a little heated in the kitchen as they were preparing one of the courses. Someone left the fish in the hotel refrigerator. When asked about it, Carl blamed his teammates instead of taking the blame. When the judges asked him why people disliked him, he basically said he didn't care what others thought. After all, he wasn't there to make friends; he was there to win the competition and win the $100,000.00.

In the end, Mike was awarded the title of "Top Chef." Even though the judges were more impressed with Carl's presentation and creativity, he lacked the people skills that would have won him the title. Carl had a very high opinion of himself and made it known that he was in it to win it...at all costs. He was not there to make friends or to be nice. Believe it or not, this is an attitude that is prevalent in many organizations, regardless of its mission.

What some people fail to realize is effective human interaction (or relationships) is essential for organizational success. Unfortunately, some people can look at themselves, see that they are negative, and choose not to do anything about it. This type of toxicity is counter-productive for team effectiveness. Before a team can be effective, every member of that team must understand who they are as a person. They must go into the closet and go through their baggage of life experiences and decipher who they are and why they think, feel, and do the things they do. This is called taking a good look at yourself.

One of the buzz words prevalent in this culture is authenticity. It is said that to be authentic is to be who you truly are without camouflaging your true identity. In his book, *Why Am I Afraid to Tell You Who I Am?*, John Powell (1995), thinks this statement can be more misleading than helpful because in his opinion, "there is no fixed, true, and real person inside you or me, precisely because being a person necessarily implies becoming a person, being in process."

He goes on to say, "If I am anything as a person, it is what I think, judge, feel, value, honor, esteem, love, hate, fear, desire, hope for, believe in, and am committed to." Powell makes an interesting point in that becoming a person is a process that is ever-changing. The person you saw yesterday is not the same person you see today because people are constantly adding to their character. As a result, I hope you are inspired to keep growing as a person, since we are all a work in progress.

Taking into consideration what you have just read, who are you and what is your purpose on the team? Different things move people to behave in a certain manner. The question, "Who Am I," is one that lingers in the minds of many people and is one that needs to be answered before you can actively participate and contribute to a team. We know the answer, but we are afraid to acknowledge or admit who we are because it may cast us in a negative light or, if revealed, may be used against us. Whether or not we know the answer, we must be honest with ourselves. To get you started, the following exercise will help you examine your thinking and behavior as it relates to your effectiveness as a team member.

EXERCISE 1

Hold a mirror to your face and answer the following questions. Do not write down what you see in a physical sense, but describe the inner person. I've included some responses others have shared just to trigger your thoughts.

1. Who do I see (the next CEO; a nice, kind-hearted person; a mean, vindictive person; etc.)?

_____

_____

_____

2. What do I see that others do not see (a nice, kind-hearted person)?

_____

_____

_____

3. How would I describe my ego? Yes, we all have one!

_____

_____

_____

4. What are my fears and why am I afraid (I was mistreated; I'm still wounded; etc.)?

_____

_____

_____

5. Why do I feel the way I feel (I'm angry; I'm bitter; I'm guilty; etc.)?

_____

_____

_____

6. Why do I react to things the way I do (I feel guilty if I don't help; I'm hurt; I'm afraid; etc.)?

_____

_____

_____

7. Why must I be in charge (gender reasons, family pressure, or cultural reasons)?

_____

_____

_____

8. What keeps me from taking the lead (other commitments, competition, or insecurity)?

_____

_____

_____

9. What is my hidden agenda?

_____

_____

_____

10. Am I the problem or the solution?

_____

_____

_____

This exercise of introspection can be frightening because it forces you to deal with the good, the bad, and the ugly that may exist within. There is a part of us that can be selfless, and in the snap of a finger become selfish. There is a part of us that can be happy for the success of a friend or family member, but in the blink of an eye become jealous or envious because it wasn't us being rewarded or recognized.

Something else that must be considered is the internal and external factors that motivate a person. For many people, the feeling of being on a team that stands for what they believe gives them a sense of satisfaction. The motivation comes from within and is referred to as an intrinsic reward. They are very powerful because of their internal nature and sustainability. In addition, these rewards drive them to a level of performance that brings a high degree of satisfaction with their work. Other examples of intrinsic rewards include competence, a sense of relevance, personal challenge, and a sense of accomplishment. Extrinsic rewards, on the other hand, are generated from outside of the individual and not obtained from the work itself. An example would include money, recognition, approval from others, bonuses, etc. Both intrinsic and extrinsic rewards affect how a person will approach a task or whether or not they want to be a part of a group effort.

Human emotions are complex and if not understood or controlled, you could find yourself on a rollercoaster that's not enjoyable. Daniel Goleman, author of the best seller *Emotional Intelligence: Why It Can Matter More than IQ*, helps us deal with some of these issues. In Chapter 4 (*Know Thyself*) of his book, he deals with this particular element of emotional intelligence–awareness of one's own feelings as they occur. Awareness of our motives and actions enable us to see why we behave in a certain manner. However, it doesn't end with awareness. You must be able and willing to halt or change that behavior, especially if it is counter-productive to team effectiveness. This is where personal accountability becomes a must if people are going to effectively work together.

What do placing blame, complaining, and procrastination have in common? A lack of personal accountability. In many leadership schools, it is taught that when things go wrong leaders should shoulder the blame. Although this is admirable, everyone should be willing to accept responsibility. According to John G. Miller (2004), author of *QBQ! The Question Behind the Question*, "personal accountability is about each of us holding ourselves accountable for our own thinking and behaviors and the results they produce." As painful as this may sound, the problem could be with us. We, as an individual, could be the one causing confusion and chaos in the office. Imagine that! There is an old saying that says, "Whenever you point a finger at a person, there are three fingers pointing back at you." This is another way of saying check yourself before you check others.

Miller's book also gives us insight into what we should ask ourselves in order to eliminate finger pointing and blaming. For example,

- Instead of asking, "Why do we have to go through this change?" Ask a better question that says, "How can I adapt to the changing world?"
- Instead of asking, "Who dropped the ball?" Ask a better question that says, "What can I do to get the project back on schedule?"

Did you notice the pronoun "I" as being part of the solution? This is something we all can do and not leave for those in leadership/management positions to fix. We have the ability to impact our office environment; therefore, we must make every effort to transform it into a place where people can learn, grow, and succeed. When we accept personal accountability, we take charge of our lives and actions and contribute towards the overall success of the organization!

Exercise 2 is an example of how a person must take ownership of the process in order for the team to succeed. As you read the exercise, place yourself in both the manager and employee's position and then answer the question that follows.

EXERCISE 2

Scenario: The weekly office meeting at Grants Department Store was not your typical, "let's all work together," meeting. Melvin, 25 years old and fresh out of grad school, was the new store manager. He replaced Mary, who had been there five years and relocated due to a promotion. John, who has been with the company for 15 years, is 55 years old and only has an 8th grade education. During the meeting, John complained about everything Melvin was not doing and why the need for change. Weeks went by and John's productivity noticeably decreased. When Melvin asked John what was going on, John responded, "What do you mean? I don't see a problem. If there is a problem, you are the problem!"

Based on what was discussed concerning "When Self Matters," what are some things Melvin and John should do to improve their working relationship?

Melvin:

_____

_____

_____

John:

_____

_____

_____

It is possible that John was offended or jealous over the fact that Melvin received the job as manager. After all, he had been with the company for 15 years.

14

Melvin should take John's feelings into consideration and try to understand how having a much younger and perhaps inexperienced manager affects John.

The aforementioned scenario happens often in organizations. Everyone wants to point the finger and blame someone else for the group's problems. Pointing fingers doesn't solve anything and only creates chaos and divisiveness. Perhaps self reflection becomes paramount, and if everyone does this and makes the necessary adjustments, then group unity can occur.

When unity is present, personal objectives become subordinate to group objectives. Members, therefore, are willing to assume whatever role necessary to ensure the group or organization succeeds. Not only do they assume necessary roles but they ask themselves, "How can I contribute to enhance the effectiveness of the organization?" This question gives birth to other questions, such as

- What do I need to do for personal or professional development?
- What are my strengths?
- What are my weaknesses?
- What must I do to function at an optimal level that moves the team or organization forward?

This type of thinking and action is contagious and can motivate others to do the same type of reflection. These high demands will often drive people of excellence to surpass the status quo and focus on what they view as success. Since the focus is on the team, these individuals will perform with excellence regardless of the role. That leads us to ask, "Do you know what your role is on the team?" The roles referred to in the next section are that of leader and follower. Both roles are critical and can be performed separately or interchangeably. The next chapter will look at the role of a leader and their responsibilities to the organization, and to those they lead.

SECTION B:

KNOW YOUR ROLES ON THE TEAM

Chapter 2: Leadership

*It is better to lead from behind and to put others
in front, especially when you celebrate victory
when nice things occur. You take the front
line when there is danger. Then people
will appreciate your leadership."*

Nelson Mandela

Leadership or the thought of being the leader can be very frightening for some people. For others, it is a role that is highly sought after or coveted. Notice I used the word role because I don't view leader as a person but as a role that a person performs. A role can be defined as a function or responsibility a person plays in a given situation. Roles are often determined or assigned by way of a formal or informal agreement. For example, there may be a set of bylaws that specifies the needed qualifications to serve in a particular role. In an informal setting, the assigning of roles can be accomplished with a verbal or consensual agreement. Both agreements can prove to be beneficial for teams that are dynamic in nature. The least ranking may be called upon to lead because of their expertise. In a situation like this, the formally designated leader willingly follows the expert because they recognize that success is most important for the group. Within a few seconds the follower transitions to serve as a leader.

The leader role is vital to the success of a group, team, or organization because the one who performs it must have the ability to influence diverse personalities to accomplish the common goal. This ought to give you an idea of what leadership is all about, because there are many definitions out there for the term. According to former Chairman of the Joint Chiefs of Staff, retired U.S. Army General Colin S. Powell, leadership is motivating people, turning people on, getting 110 percent out of a personal relationship (Harari, 2005).

During my tenure in the Air Force, leadership was drilled into our heads from day one. There is a misconception that military leadership is only one way, that being top-down leadership. Contrary to this belief, at least in the Air Force, leadership has come to recognize the significant value that subordinates bring to the table. Depending on the situation, an individual may have to take an order and salute smartly. That basically means carrying out the orders of those in command whether you agree or disagree. However, those who understand good leadership, lead in a way that allows two-way communication when the situation warrants it.

Since leadership is such a broad topic, let's narrow our focus and examine the relational aspects of leadership. I'll begin with this quote:

> *Good leaders are people who have a strong passion to succeed... To become successful leaders, we must first learn that no matter how good the technology or how shiny the equipment, people-to-people relations get things done in our organizations. People are the assets that determine our success or failure. If you are to be a good leader, you have to cultivate your skills in the arena of personal relations.*
>
> *General Ronald R. Fogleman,*
> *Former Air Force Chief of Staff*

As a leader, you must understand your responsibilities as it relates to people. While speaking to a group of middle school students, I asked who wants to be a leader. A young girl raised her hand and I asked her why. She stated she wanted to tell people what to do! I thought this was a rather interesting response because I've met many people in my career, who thought this is what leadership was about. For some strange reason, bossing people around seems to excite some individuals. Could it be they were bullied as a child or picked upon by their older siblings? I could never figure this out because these same people don't like it when other people tell them what to do. This is one of those moments that make you say "hmmm."

True leadership, however, is about relationships and influence. The relationship you have with those who follow you is crucial to your success as a leader. I attended a leadership seminar and the speaker was a store manager from a large department store. He spoke on the in-depth leadership training he received and how the company recognized the importance of this role. He indicated that the company's leadership team is a strong proponent of the 360 degree feedback whereby the leader receives feedback from his or her subordinates, peers, and superiors. The company also requires its leaders to accept this constructive feedback and make the necessary adjustments that will produce positive outcomes. This is a very tough assignment because of the diverse personalities and needs that a leader encounters. It comes down to becoming all things to all people, so that you may gain their trust and support.

Another aspect of relational leadership that should be considered is why do people follow you? According to John Maxwell (2001), *Developing the Leader Within You, people follow because*

1. they have to,
2. they want to,
3. of what the leader has done for the organization,
4. of what the leader has done for them personally,
5. of who the leader is and what the leader represents,

John Maxwell makes some very valid points. The leader's job becomes a little tougher when a person is only following because they feel they have no choice. The reasons they feel forced to follow could be due to an economic downturn, financial obligations, or family obligations. Therefore, it becomes even more critical for leaders, who have those who fit into the "I have to follow you" category, reach out to them and make a connection. Leaders should not resort to intimidation, threats, abuse, or retaliation against those who are forced to follow them. Instead, good leaders will use their emotional intelligence to empathize with them to discover or create a common bond.

Speaking on emotional intelligence, a study was done that revealed some people who possess high IQ's fail on their jobs because they lack interpersonal skills. Claudio Fernández-Aráoz, a social scientist, found in an analysis of new c-level executives that those who had been hired for their self-discipline, drive, and intellect were sometimes later fired for lacking basic social skills. In other words, the people Fernández-Aráoz studied had smarts in spades, but their inability to get along socially on the job was professionally self-defeating (Goleman, 2008). Dr. Daniel Goleman, a renowned psychologist and leading advocate of emotional intelligence, believes emotional intelligence is more of an accurate measurement in determining a person's ability to succeed or fail. Emotional intelligence examines five categories of personal and social competence. The personal includes self awareness, self-regulation, and motivation. The social includes understanding others and managing relationships. Leading effectively is, in other words, less about mastering situations— or even mastering social skill sets—than it is about developing a genuine interest in and talent for fostering positive feelings in the people whose cooperation and support you need (Goleman, 2008). Taking this into consideration, I offer the following advice to leaders:

Remember your past. Recall what it was like to be on the other side of the table facing the leader. Were you afraid or intimidated? Did you feel like you could tell your leader anything without being ridiculed or shut down?

Recognize that those who follow you are people. People have feelings and emotions. Learn what motivates them. What are their aspirations? What are their strengths and areas for improvement?

Make excellence mandatory. Followers respect leaders who see the best in them. They appreciate and want to know that you desire their very best.

Be human. Because of your exceptional skills and abilities, they may view you as a super hero. Let them know you care, have feelings or even have those days where you don't have a clue.

Be firm yet gentle. Some people want a leader who is straight forward, but even those people must be spoken to with respect. It also means being strong and not passive.

Exude confidence. People are looking to you for guidance, strength, and reassurance that things are going to work out.

Never assume people should know better. This is a big mistake for some leaders. Recognize that everyone has not been exposed to your upbringing, environment, training, and situations in life. As a result, they may not know any better.

Educate and facilitate. Teach people what you know then allow them to teach you what they know!

Demand competence. People may come in not knowing how to do something, but they should never be allowed to remain not knowing anything. Do not tolerate incompetence.

Demonstrate your appreciation. All work and no play can knock the wind out of a person's sail. Make time with your team to have fun and enjoy the wonderful experiences life has to offer. You can't afford not to!

Do not accept blind obedience. If people agree with everything you say, you are in trouble. Cultivate an environment where people are free to respectfully and courageously disagree and provide viable solutions. The key is to allow your team to be heard and recognize their value to the process.

These are just a few things that you as a leader can do to create synergy and excitement among those you lead. This next task, however, is something that will not only benefit your team members but you as well. It is the task of delegation. By delegating tasks to others, you can then take on more advanced tasks that will prepare you for future opportunities. Another reason why you delegate tasks is so you can develop yourself for future promotions and career opportunities. More importantly, it helps develop the followers behind you to fill the void when you are promoted. Here are seven steps to delegating tasks to achieve success:

Understand the task. Make sure you understand the task, so that you can clearly communicate it to the person asked to perform the task. You must also understand what resources are required to succeed, and what tools you have to make the task successful. If your team members are not progressing on the task, what options do you have as a leader and manager to make it successful?

Find the right person. Find the person who is motivated to take on the task. You may have someone who has the skills but is not motivated to do it.

26

However, if you have someone that doesn't have the skills but is highly motivated to learn and is excited about the opportunity, then this is a good candidate for delegation.

Communicate the task. Take the time to clearly communicate the task and the expectations. Most importantly, communicate the ownership of the task. This means that the person assigned to the task will be ultimately responsible for its success. When communicating responsibility for the task, let the person know the consequences of not completing it and the rewards for completing it. If possible, show the employee how to do the task because telling and showing enhances the probability of his/her understanding and being confident with the task.

Provide resources, remove barriers. Whether it is the time, people, or technology, it is the leader's responsibility to ensure the person is set up for success.

Guarantee understanding. Make sure when the person leaves the meeting that he/she understands exactly what is expected. The typical interaction between a manager or supervisor and the employee is the manager asks, "Do you understand everything we discussed?" The employee of course says, "Yes." Then a week later, the manager is disappointed with the results of the task and asks, "What happened?" The employee says, "I didn't understand what I was supposed to do." By asking the question differently, "Mike, please share with me your understanding of

Jef Williams

what is required to make this task successful," the
person giving the answer is required to give a com-
prehensive answer detailing their thoughts on the
task at hand.

Encourage success. Let the person know that you
have confidence in them. Remember, in most cases,
this task is new to them and by communicating that
you are confident that he/she will be successful gives
them the confidence to succeed.

Follow-up, reward, follow-up, reward.

- Make sure you know the level of follow-up required. Some people may want much follow-
  up, while other may require little. It depends
  on the complexity of the task.
- Have scheduled follow-ups.
- Reward progress at each follow-up meeting in
  public if possible. Show your appreciation in
  the meeting, so that everyone is motivated to
  do more.
- Correct to get back on track. This may be as
  simple as showing the correct way or simply
  brainstorming for possible solutions.

As a leader, you will realize that effective delegation helps you accomplish more and also allows your
team members to learn this skill set as well. Don't
be surprised if those you lead begin to mimic your
style.

The Model

The leader is a model for their followers. Every time you enter the room, you are on the runway and they are watching you from head to toe. They observe what you have on, how you walk, how you talk, what you are eating, your attitude for the moment, and how you respond to situations. Yes, you are under a microscope. Followers also watch how their leaders follow leaders. As a result, it is imperative that you model the type of followership you desire in your followers.

If you want excellence, then you must model excellence. If you want people to be a problem solver, then you must show them the process for solving problems. Also, you can't assume people will view things the way you view them. Here's the perfect example. A father was walking throughout his house and noticed a stench coming from his son's room. What could that awful smell be? He opened the door and noticed a bowl of something that had enough mold in it to grow penicillin. There were old soda cans throughout the room. The clean clothes were being held hostage by the dirty clothes. There was dust on the headboard and dresser. The further he went into the room, the more he realized his life was in danger. He stumbled over some wet sneakers and realized what the culprit was. The wet sneakers smelled so bad that it could unclog one's sinuses. As the father continued through this madness, the son walked in and proceeded to make himself comfortable. How? God only knows.

Anyway, the father tells the son to pick up this mess. The son cleaned the room. The father went back into the room and noticed the room was not clean. The son had pushed things under the bed, picked some clothes and trash up from the floor and that was it. This happened on several occasions until the father asked, "Do you understand what clean the room means?" The son replied, "Yes. Your clean and my clean are two different things." The father took in a deep breath, and instead of flying off the deep end, he said, "you are correct. Our definitions of clean are totally different. However, since you live in my house and don't pay rent, you must clean this room according to my definition." The father then showed the son what a clean room looked like by literally helping the son clean the room. When it was done, the father said, this is what I mean by clean. Do you understand son? The son quickly understood.

Similar situations happen when leaders expect their people to know about the leader's idiosyncrasies. Be clear on what you expect and then model the expected behavior. Your modeling is setting the atmosphere that will determine the office's health.

Set the Atmosphere
Since, leaders set the tone or the atmosphere of the office or environment, the tone you set is important because some people tend to do as much or

as little as you allow. In their book, *Pygmalion in the Classroom,* Rosenthal and Jacobson (1992) talk about a phenomenon known as the Pygmalion Effect. It has been studied that the greater the expectation placed upon people, the greater they perform. With this in mind, what type of environment have you established? Are people afraid of you? Do people present ideas or simply do as you tell them? This is where some of the negative stereotypes of being a follower come from.

When followers do not step up or simply do as told, it is automatically assumed that they lack initiative and competence. The problem could be the leader and their unwillingness to allow their followers to be vocal, creative, or even take charge. Some wield their power to hold back rewards, to discipline, or to terminate those who oppose them, which in turn causes some followers to be docile. The lack of delegation and autonomy can be stifling to where it shuts down communication and innovation. According to Chaleff (2009),

> The new power of customers and constituents makes it imperative for organizations to develop cultures in which candid conversations can first occur *within* the organization. Leaders must hear and understand what those closest to their constituents and markets know. *How can we ensure that senior leaders hear what they need to in large organizations when they are*

many levels removed from those who can best inform them?

So again, what type of atmosphere have you established? This is an important question because good followership hinges on whether leadership will allow it to exist. Reflect on this quote as we proceed to the next chapter on followership.

"Leadership is the ability to establish standards and manage a creative climate where people are self-motivated toward the mastery of long term constructive goals, in a participatory environment of mutual respect, compatible with personal values."

— Mike Vance

Chapter 3: Followership: The Reason for Leadership

"Followership, like leadership, is a role and not a destination."

Michael McKinney

Throughout my 26 years in the military, I often wondered, what it takes to be a great leader. As I advanced through the ranks, it became evident that most of my learning of leadership came when I was in the second chair. Today when people ask that question, I respond by saying, "Learn how to be a great follower!" This is not something you would hear in our culture, but the truth of the matter is, we all serve in this role regardless of our position in an organization. When I served as an assistant I was able to observe, listen, analyze, and anticipate the actions of the leader. Serving in this follower role provided a safety net for me to learn and make mistakes in the process without bringing harm to the team. As mentioned previously, the term follower doesn't have the same appeal as the term leader. To prove this point, list five negative stereotypes associated with the term follower.

_____

_____

_____

Negative terms such as flunky, gopher, yes-person, and weak are what prevent us from acknowledging the true meaning of the follower role. Regardless of what people may say, the role itself is just as powerful as the leader's role. Former Chairman of the Joint Chiefs of Staff, Gen Colin Power says it this way, "Leadership is all about followership. You aren't really a leader if no one is willing to follow you." He goes on to say, "this is not rocket science, but in this day and age where people are consumed with titles and status, this little known fact is often pushed to the side." There is also an old African proverb that says,

If you go for a walk in the bush and after a short time you look around and the people of your village are also going for a walk along the same path then you are a leader. If you

go for a walk in the bush and after a short time you look around and there is no one behind you then you are just going for a walk.

In case you hadn't noticed, the determining factor for being a leader is having followers. Failure to acknowledge this important ingredient would be detrimental to the morale and success of any organization. Like leadership, it cannot be treated as a stand-alone topic; followership must be viewed alongside its counterpart. According to *Warren Bennis,* distinguished professor *at the* University of Southern California and author of *Leaders and On Becoming A Leader,* "In many ways, great followership is harder than leadership. It has more dangers and few rewards, and it must routinely be exercised with much more subtlety. But great followership has never been more important."

The question that begs to be answered is, "What is followership?" The root word of course is follower. While most people would hold on to the negative stereotype of this term, Chaleff (2003), in his book entitled *The Courageous Follower – Standing Up To and For Our Leaders,* defines followers as more than subordinates. A subordinate reports to an individual of higher rank and may in practice be a supporter, an antagonist, or indifferent; but a true follower shares a common purpose with the leader, believes in what the organization is trying to accomplish, and wants both the leader and the organization to succeed.

Examples of those who by definition can be considered followers:

Secretary of State	Secretary of Defense
Senators	Congressmen
Generals	Colonels
Lieutenants	Chief Master Sergeants
CEO	President
Vice Presidents	Directors
Managers	Supervisors
Team Leaders	Pastors
Deacons	Church Members
Superintendents	Administrators
Administrators	Teachers

You will never hear individuals, such as congressmen, generals, superintendents, or pastors referred to as followers, even though they all follow the lead of another. Secretary of State Hillary Rodham Clinton is one of the most powerful people in the world, yet she still must be a follower to the president. Follower is not her title; it's simply something she does in relation to the leader.

People will insist on changing the term follower. This could be done if we eliminate the term leader. Like you, I don't see this happening anytime soon, so let's embrace the term follower for what it is…a role that we all perform in our daily activities. Followership, as stated in the Merriam-Webster Online dictionary, is the capacity and willingness to follow a leader. Per the Reverend Paul Beedle, "Followership is a discipline of supporting leaders and helping them to lead well. It is not submission, but the wise and good care of leaders, done out of a sense of gratitude for their willingness to take on the responsibilities of leadership, and a sense of hope and faith in their abilities and potential."

Bearing these definitions in mind, list five positive terms associated with the word follower.

_____

_____

_____

Next, I want you to review the five negative and five positive terms you wrote regarding followers. Why do people insist on avoiding the use of the term follower when it is evident that followers make positive contributions to the team? Personal and cultural biases play a role on a person's perspectives. Nevertheless, when viewed in a positive manner, the role of the follower is critical.

For many years, companies have invested in the development of its leaders and soon to be leaders. Many hours are spent on how to lead. What happens in many cases is people forget the importance of following. In addition, those in non-leadership roles are left in the wind with a feeling of neglect. The reality of this situation is that leadership roles are few and everyone will not have the opportunity to serve in a leadership role as viewed by society. Another fact that we often overlook is that not everyone wants to be the leader.

Do You Want to Lead?

I recall giving a presentation to some mid-level managers, and I asked the following question: "How many of you want to be a supervisor or manager?" Only 30 percent of the people expressed interest in being in a leadership role. The other 70 percent indicated they were in the position because they didn't have a choice, or they needed the money to make ends meet. Additionally, some didn't want to be in a leadership role because they enjoyed working in the background and giving the needed support. Others stated they valued their personal time and weren't willing to sacrifice it for a leadership position. Another stated they were leading in another organization and did not want to assume an additional leadership role.

Amazingly, these individuals were well capable of serving as a leader but chose not to. Should we look down upon these individuals? Of course not! It would be better to put people who are willing and able into roles they want to perform, instead of roles that they don't want or are forced to perform. This is an overlooked reality and makes the discussion on followership very important.

Chapter 4: Followership Explored

"It is the men behind who make the man ahead."

Merle Crowell

Why Followership?

As mentioned earlier, followership is an unspoken reality that must be brought to the forefront of all discussions pertaining to leadership. Followership development is essential because it's the foundation of leadership. Many would agree that before one can lead, one must know how to follow. Followership defines what it means to follow, and then prepares those who master this skill to perform in an exemplary manner whether in preparation for a leadership role or support role.

I find it interesting that when a child begins to form complete sentences or thoughts, they have no problem giving orders. The difficulty comes when the parent begins teaching them how to take or follow orders. Some would refer to this stage as the terrible two's. They are very bossy. It's their way and no other way. Understanding followership begins early in life, and must be reinforced throughout life, if there is to be any chance for order or civility. The child must understand what it means to follow before he or she can demand others to follow them.

A great leader who knew the importance of followership is Thomas Jefferson. Greg Thomas (2003), founder and CEO of weLEAD Incorporated, points out,

> Most people would look upon the accomplishments of Thomas Jefferson and immediately recognize his effective multifaceted leadership skills. However, in 1776 and at the age of 33, Jefferson played a *follower's* role as part of a *committee* established to create the United States *Declaration of Independence*. Dwarfed by other powerful committee members such as Benjamin Franklin and John Adams, he quietly drafted the document as a *junior* member of the committee. His authorship was little known outside of the Continental Congress and he received no public recognition until eight years afterward when it was revealed in a newspaper article. This significant contribution of a *follower* helped to change world history and the experience he gained from observing

his senior committee members prepared him
for <u>future</u> leadership responsibilities.

Followership development also provides leaders with a team of dedicated, mission-focused, and
result oriented individuals who prefer to support
and protect the leader. Yes, there are many people
who believe their purpose in life is the gift of service.
Notice, I said the gift of service. These are individuals, who with all their heart enjoy serving others who
are in leadership positions or their peers.

Another point that should not go unnoticed is
the label placed upon those who may be performing
in a negative or subpar manner. It's amazing that
when a person is performing in a negative manner,
they say that person is just a follower. However, when
the person begins to perform in an excellent manner
they call them a leader. This is the typical attitude
that perpetuates the negative stereotype of the term
follower and one that must be corrected.

The act of following is something we all do regardless of the position or title we possess. A supervisor
follows the manager. The manager follows the director. The director follows the vice president. The
vice president follows the president. The president
answers to its board of directors. These are all leadership roles and yet they still must master the art of
followership.

We are all followers in one way or another. The
question then becomes, how do we follow? In the early

1990's, Robert E. Kelley, a noted social scientist on follow-ership studies, conducted preliminary research on the styles of followership. According to Kelley (2008), two dimensions define the way people follow: (1) Do they think for themselves, and (2) Are they actively engaged in creating positive energy for the organization. Based on these dimensions, the following styles evolved:

The Passive or Sheep. These individuals look to the leader to think for them and to motivate them. For example, you can assign a task to this person and they will only do what is requested of them. They will do the bare minimum and will not take the initiative to do more than what is asked.

The Conformist or Yes-People. They are positive, always on the leader's side, but look to the leader to do the thinking for them. These individuals want to be on the leader's good side and believe by not oppos-ing the leader, the leader will show favor towards them. If the leader says, "Let's jump off the build-ing," the yes person will say it sounds like a great idea.

The Alienated. They think for themselves, but have a lot of negative energy. They are not moving in a positive direction. These individuals are not in line with the leader or the team because they may have been rejected by the leader or have a different agenda. They are very critical of the leader's agenda and will not provide solutions or recommendations that could further the team's objectives.

The Pragmatics. They sit on the fence to see which way things are headed before they get on board. These individuals also prefer to keep things the way they are and operate with the mindset that they will outlast the leader.

The Exemplary or Star Followers. They think for themselves, are very active, and have positive energy. They do not accept the leader's decision without their own independent evaluation of its soundness. If they disagree with the leader, they will provide other alternatives for consideration. These individuals can easily transition to the leadership role while simultaneously performing in their follower role.

Kelley's work allows us to see the various dimensions to followership orientations, and should serve as an eye-opener because there is more to the term follower than one who is passive or just stands by and waits for instruction. Though unfortunate, this is the behavior that comes to mind when most people think of the term follower. What's also quite interesting to discover is that there are categories to describe how people follow. Something that must be stated unequivocally is that these styles do not define a person. They simply describe how one may perform or behave in a particular situation or environment. In addition, several factors should be taken into account before labeling a person.

   a. The leader's style of leadership – micro-manager, hands-off, participative, or delegator
   b. The individual's attitude and self perceptions – self esteem, ego, elitism, gender, past abuse (mental or physical)

    c. The setting – small business, large business, formal or informal

    d. The relationship of the parties concerned – family ran business, friendly, relaxed, no nonsense

    e. Organizational culture – hierarchical, flat, informal

    f. Experience level – apprentice, very skilled

To expound upon this point, I will provide two examples as to why a person may be a passive follower. The first scenario involves a person who is new to a particular process. If they have no prior experience in performing this task or if the directions are unclear or ambiguous, they may wait to be told what to do and how to do it, to avoid bringing harm to the organization or embarrassment to themselves. The second scenario involves a person who has no desire to assume responsibility or accountability. They are content with being told what to do and how to do it.

During a seminar, the following question was asked of the attendees, "Which of Kelley's followership styles describe you?" Many stated they find themselves in all five styles depending on the situation. Many people would love to say they are exemplary followers 100 percent of the time. If truth be told, we all at times become alienated when leaders offend us and/or take advantage of us. It's human nature. The goal however, is to be able to function as an effective or exemplary follower and have the courage to confront leaders when offenses or behaviors that are counterproductive to organizational success occur.

Exemplary Followership

The power of leadership lies in its followership. Merle Crowell, long time editor of American Magazine, says it this way, "It is the men behind who make the man ahead." Exemplary followers possess a skill set that complements the leader and together they form a dynamic team that produces dynamic results. According to Kelley (2008), some people view these people as "leaders in disguise," but this is basically because those people have a hard time accepting that followers can display such independence and positive behavior. Exemplary followers, or star followers, are often referred to as "my right-hand person" or my "go-to person."

Roman philosopher and statesman, Cicero, also recognized the importance of this type of followership. He stated, "If a man aspires to the highest place, it is no dishonor to him to halt at the second." To be referred to as "my right-hand person" or "my go-to person" is a title that propels a person to the next level. Exemplary followers can also be viewed as the leader's trusted agent, moral conscience, or as a dynamic force in the workplace. It is an honor to be recognized as such and it is not a title that comes easily. What must an individual do to warrant such recognition? They must perform in a manner that exemplifies the term "followership."

Chapter 5: Terminology of Exemplary Followership

Based on my research and personal experience, the individual who possesses the characteristics of an exemplary or effective follower is someone who is a self-motivated, high performance individual who shares the vision and the responsibility of goal achievement with the leader. This individual is also someone who courageously supports and holds accountable their leader, and other team members, through their acts of selflessness, integrity, and their own capacity to lead.

The following qualities are common among those who exhibit exemplary followership behavior:

Respectful. They respect and understand the pressures placed upon leaders and do what they can to help shoulder the burden and face the challenge. They are encouragers, protectors, and supporters.

Professional. They have the etiquette to convey "confidence, assurance, interest, and respect (Bovée, 2005)." The manner in which a person presents themselves is critical. Communication experts Bovee and Thill (2005) also believe communication skills are critical when interacting with leaders. In addition, being properly dressed and groomed indicates respect and consideration for the organization and those whom they work with.

Integrity. Being honest to the leader and to the team. Practices good behavior and accepts responsibility for their shortcomings. They do what is right, especially when no one is looking.

Competent. Displaying the critical and analytical skills necessary to perform that job in a spirit of excellence.

Vision-minded. The ability to recognize the vision and use it as a guide to determine work behavior and decisions that affect the organization.

Initiative. The ability to start an action to include coming up with an idea and giving or helping without first being requested to do so.

Team oriented. Personal needs become secondary for the sake of the team. They are viewed as effective collaborators and accountability partners.

Loyalty. Sacrificing one's wishes and time in favor of the leader's needs, vision, and support. They protect the leader and other team members from being blind-sided, from gossip and anything that could harm the team. Colin Powell views loyalty as such:

"When we are debating an issue, loyalty means giving me your honest opinion, whether you think I'll like it or not. Disagreement, at this stage, stimulates me. But once a decision has been made, the debate ends. From that point on, loyalty means executing the decision as if it were your own."

Commitment. They have complete devotion to duty. They do their best under any condition when performing assigned duties. According to Thomas (2003), "Often times the best efforts of followers may not be what are most needed or expedient for a given situation. Wise followers accept this fact and continue to make significant contributions to the organization because they want what is best for the organization rather than their own ego."

Self-motivated. They are moved by internal factors such as their morals, beliefs and integrity.

Innovative. Use of imagination to create new products, ideas, or solutions that would benefit the organization.

Powerful. They have influential relationships or networks that reach beyond the immediate team and in many cases beyond the organization.

Autonomy. They can perform without supervision. They smartly handle authority that has been delegated and will always act responsibly.

Partners/Collaborators. They see themselves as colleagues, equal contributors to the mission.

Exceptional interpersonal skills. They have the ability to interact and relate with other people regardless of their gender, age, nationality, etc.

Courageous. Not afraid to assume responsibility, courage to serve and to challenge, courage to participate in change and to stay the course during transformation (Chaleff, 2003).

These are just a few descriptors of exemplary followers. I intentionally listed courage as the last item because I believe one must have courage to perform as a change agent, to take the initiative, to exhibit loyalty, integrity and commitment. Courage, in my opinion, is the foundation of exemplary followership. Chaleff (2003), views courageous followership in five dimensions:

1. Courage to assume responsibility - They discover or create opportunities to fulfill their potential and maximize their value to the organization.
2. Courage to serve – They are not afraid of the hard work required to serve a leader; they assume new or additional responsibilities to unburden the leader and serve the organization.
3. Courage to challenge – They are willing to stand up, to stand out, to risk rejection, to initiate conflict in order to examine the actions of the leader and group when appropriate.
4. Courage to participate in transformation – They champion the need for change and stay with the leader and group while they mutually struggle with the difficulty of real change.

5. Courage to take moral action - They know when it is time to take a stand that is different than that of the leader's because they are answering to a higher set of values (Chaleff 2003).

Like Kelley, Chaleff also developed a typology of followers and based it on the dimensions of courage to support the leader and the courage to challenge the leader's behavior or policies:

1. Resource – This individual will do only what is required to retain their position.
2. Individualist – This person will speak up when no one else will and will often be marginalized because they are too contrary.
3. Implementer – The leader prefers this style but runs the risk of making mistakes because this individual will not caution them against said mistakes.
4. Partner – This person assumes total responsibility for their and the leader's behavior and then acts accordingly.

Occasions will arise where an individual is faced with the decision to follow the masses or do the right thing. There have been reported cases of widespread corruption among the leadership in organizations and because of fear of retribution, it was allowed to continue. There have also been reported cases of corruption among employees, and because of the fear of being ostracized or labeled as a stool pigeon, the behavior was again allowed to continue. In both cases, courage was needed to make a change for the better.

As you may have noticed, effective followership is a huge responsibility and takes courage. Now that you are armed with this new information, answer the following questions by taking an honest look at your followership style.

EXERCISE 3:

1. Which of Kelley's five types best describe your followership style?

_____

_____

_____

2. For those who serve in a leadership position (supervisor, manager, teacher, director, president, vice president, etc.) which of Kelley's five types best describe how you follow your leader?

_____

_____

_____

3. When serving in the follower role, what are you willing to do to ensure integrity is maintained and organizational objectives are achieved?

_____

_____

_____

The first two questions are the same yet worded differently to convey that regardless of the title or position that we hold, following is a function that we routinely perform. If your long term goal is to be an effective leader you must be an effective follower. What changes will you make to ensure your goal is met? In the next chapter, we further explore how an individual shifts between the leader and follower roles.

Chapter 6: The Leader-Follower: Two Roles in One

"Followership is not only a prerequisite to leadership; it is also a continuing role. Exemplary followers demonstrate an ability to become good leaders— while continuing to be good followers."

Patrick L. Townsend and Joan E. Gephardt

Depending on the type of organizational structure, a person can find themselves serving in both leader and follower roles. A manager can lead or oversee five different departments and still follow or report to the vice president of operations. To perform these two roles effectively, the manager must exhibit those traits that are exemplary in nature. The following chart reflects traits that are found in both exemplary leaders and followers:

EXEMPLARY LEADERS	EXEMPLARY FOLLOWERS
Courageous	Courageous
Visionary	Vision-Minded
Integrity	Integrity
Competent	Competent
Respectful	Respectful
Inspiring	Inspiring
Imaginative	Imaginative

A mid-level manager is a prime example of an individual who simultaneously serves as both a leader and follower. In one role the manager demonstrates courage as a follower when it comes to interacting with the senior executive staff and in some cases may challenge some initiatives that may not prove beneficial to the organization, especially the front line employees. But, in the leader role, the manager demonstrates courage to gain the respect of his/her employees. It takes courage to be able to orchestrate the actions of diverse personalities. Notice, we have the same person performing different roles in different situations. The beauty of this role shift is it can be effortless when the ego is in check. With ego in check, the manager is basically saying, "I'm good at whatever role I'm playing because the goal is to succeed and achieve our objectives." This also describes what Gene Dixon calls the Leader-Follower Organization.

According to Dixon (2008), the leader-follower organization is the organic state in which all organization members are capable of transitioning between leading and following throughout the scope of their responsibilities. Even though it is not verbalized, the reality is that this is occurring in many organizations. He also notes that the dual role of a person who is both follower and leader demonstrates an art form where the individual moves fluidly between these two roles and remains consistent in his or her treatment of others.

To explain this in another manner, let's use a sports analogy. To all the sports fans, if I were to ask who is considered the leader while on the football field, what would be your response? The quarterback would be the most logical response. The quarterback's vision is to win the game and the way they lead the team is by executing plays that will allow them to score in the end zone. In the same breath, the quarterback is also viewed as a follower because he must follow the game plan that may have been drafted by the offensive coordinator and/or head coach. I remember watching the movie, *Remember the Titans*, starring Denzel Washington. He was an African American, no-nonsense, and very aggressive head coach brought in during a time of racial segregation. His team was racially divided; yet, he demanded excellence from all those affiliated with the team, to include the coaching staff. It was his way or no way. This style of leadership may have been effective starting out to bring the team together, but as the story unfolded, it turned out to be a problem.

In one scene, Denzel clashed with the defensive coordinator because the Titans were not preventing the other team from scoring. After a heated conversation, a change takes place between the two. With the game on the line a decision had to be made. Denzel, the no-nonsense, my way or the highway coach, had to make a decision to lead or to follow the expertise of the defensive coordinator. He followed the advice of the defensive coordinator and as a result, the Titans regained possession, scored and won the game.

This is just another example of how one person can shift between the leader and follower role. The head coach did not give up his position as the head coach. With ego aside, he simply decided to play a different role, so that the team could win. The question then becomes, can this type of exchange take place between anyone? I would say "no" because it requires a level of trust and respect between both parties. It requires both parties to perform in a manner that exudes excellence. It requires setting aside the over-inflated ego for the sake and welfare of the team.

There will be times when this shifting of roles between leader and follower is difficult. Your desires may conflict with those of the leader and vice versa. An example of this is the conflict that took place between President Harry S. Truman and General

Douglas MacArthur in regards to the military strategy used during the Korean War. The following is just a portion of the address of the president which was broadcasted from the White House and released on April 11, 1951:

> I believe that we must try to limit the war to Korea for these vital reasons: to make sure that the precious lives of our fighting men are not wasted; to see that the security of our country and the free world is not needlessly jeopardized; and to prevent a third world war. A number of events have made it evident that General MacArthur did not agree with that policy. I have therefore considered it essential to relieve General MacArthur so that there would be no doubt or confusion as to the real purpose and aim of our policy.
>
> It was with the deepest personal regret that I found myself compelled to take this action. General MacArthur is one of our greatest military commanders. But the cause of world peace is more important than any individual. (pbs.org)

Positive conflict is healthy. It's what generates brilliant ideas and solutions. But when it undermines authority and results in insubordination, then one of two things should happen. The follower, which in this case is General MacArthur, needed to do what we call in the military, salute smartly and carry out the orders of those appointed over him. If this cannot be done for whatever reason, then one should willingly resign from the team because it becomes apparent that your values differ from that of the organization or leadership. Because of his views and his actions, the general was removed. Even senior leaders must remember the importance of exemplary followership.

On several occasions, I attended the A-Staff (C-Suite) meeting which was comprised of the senior leaders on the military installation. These individuals were the directors of the different organizations and normally held the rank of colonels (0-6), SES – which is the civilian equivalent to a general officer, and other general officers. The commander was a 4-star general and was THE LEADER! I was fortunate, as a chief master sergeant, to be on the sidelines as an observer. There was a lot of power in the room because these were leaders among leaders. They were also followers because they followed the command of the 4-star general.

I knew some of these individuals on a professional basis and noticed how they led when they were in their organizations. When they walked into the room, however, you knew who was in charge based on their rank and their demeanor. I did notice a difference when these high ranking leaders were in the presence of the LEADER…the 4-star general. Some had no problem courageously disagreeing with the

4-star and sharing information that was not what the general wanted to hear. On the other-hand, there were some who chose not to disagree and preferred to simply find a way to appease the general. Why do I point out this scenario? To show the importance of being an exemplary leader and follower at all times. Whether leading or following, someone is watching your every move and how you respond in certain situations. Not only are people modeling you as a leader, they are also modeling your style of followership. Your actions will determine how people follow you as a leader. And, your actions can determine how people will lead others.

Let me close with a personal testimony. I was fortunate to work with and for an individual who epitomizes the essence of leadership-followership. When it came time to stand up against counter-productive practices, he would do so even if it risked him being marginalized, chastised, or even alienated. At all times he would give his honest and professional opinion. Even when it was not accepted, he still saluted smartly and supported his leadership.

As I witnessed this first hand, he let me know that this was the type of support he wanted in his staff. I was allowed to openly share my ideas and even express my opposition to certain plans or strategies. Just like him, I demonstrated courage and respect for leadership. It doesn't stop there. Those who followed me noticed the mutual respect in the relationship I had with my supervisor. They modeled my behavior and realized that this is what I desired from them. I wanted them to tell me if I was missing the mark; and if so, what was needed to get back on track. They knew that I valued healthy conflict and felt courageous enough to give it to me.

While being confident, a leader must also be humble enough to realize they don't know it all and cannot survive without the support of a good team of dedicated and competent members. It's when the two (leaders and followers) become one team that success is in sight! In the next chapter, we will review the dynamics of this relationship.

Chapter 7: The Leader-Follower Relationship

"The most important single ingredient in the formula of success is knowing how to get along with people."

Theodore Roosevelt

The ability for leaders and followers to work harmoniously is what also defines a dynamic team. Whether small, medium, or large, teamwork is necessary to ensure the shared vision is achieved. Cross & Parker (2004) stated that the traditional organizational hierarchy between leaders and followers has eroded over time thanks to expanding social networks and the growing empowerment of followers through their ability to access information more easily. The advent of the information age has highlighted the need for flexible leader-follower relationships.

In the beginning of this book, it was necessary to take a good look within, because before a person can contribute to the team, they must know what they can contribute. A person must recognize whether or not what they bring to the team takes away from the effectiveness of the team or enhances its effectiveness. The discussion about the ego was deliberate, because in order to function on a dynamic team that requires the shifting between roles, one's ego must be in check. A person with an inflated ego must be willing to deflate for the sake of the team. Maintaining an inflated ego takes away from the team because it often causes strife among members. People will often take offense to those who go out of their way to make it seem as though they are "God's gift to the world." When this occurs, other team members will avoid this person and the team may miss the opportunity of benefiting from what that person could otherwise bring to the team.

I recall a situation that occurred while I was working in a legal office. The staff was extremely busy working on a court case. The paralegals were swamped handling witness issues and ensuring records for the trial were processed in a timely manner. As the phones were ringing and stress level were rising, a young attorney walked pass the copier machine and asked an already busy paralegal to make a single copy of a document. The paralegal responded and said, "Sir, could you make the copy because I am swamped with these other issues?" The attorney responded, "I didn't go to law school to make copies." The look of disbelief was all over the paralegal's face. Unfortunately, word about the incident travelled throughout the office and the battle lines between the professional staff (attorneys) and support staff (paralegals) were drawn. It was "us vs. them." You may have had a thought of disbelief as you read through this story. In the next exercise, review the questions and provide your assessment of the situation.

EXERCISE 4:

1. How would you characterize the behavior or attitude of the leader (attorney)?

_____

_____

_____

2. If you were the paralegal, what would have been your response to the attorney?

_____

_____

_____

3. What affect do you think this incident had on the office members?

_____

_____

_____

4. What else could the paralegal or attorney have done in this situation to prevent a schism amongst the team?

_____

_____

_____

I can only imagine what some of you may have said regarding the attitude of the attorney. Some may think the paralegal would be justified in giving the attorney a piece of his/her mind. However, if this were done, it could have been grounds for the para-legal to be reprimanded or fired for insubordination. A situation like this can be very volatile, so it is impor-tant for one or both parties to exhibit some degree of emotional intelligence. Courage, along with respect is needed for the paralegal to confront what may appear to be an attitude of elitism. The focus should be upon how it made you feel and the effect it could have on the effectiveness of the team. If this doesn't work, the paralegal may have to bring it to the attention of a senior member and hopefully, that person will agree that this behavior is not welcomed.

Another example of leader-follower relationships can be found within the Department of Defense (DoD). The DoD is comprised of civilians, military officers and enlisted members. These groups make up the military team; and it is important that they understand and respect what each brings to the team. In the officer and enlisted relationship, the officer is recognized as the leader because of their status as an officer. Officers are given the authority to issue lawful orders and enlisted members swear or affirm, during their oath of enlistment, to obey such orders. You may have an enlisted person that has been in the military for many years, yet they are still required to follow the lead of a second lieutenant who has been in the military for just a few months.

There are cases where the officers and enlisted members exhibit the leadership-followership state paradigm. Ernest L. Stech (2008), author of *A New Leadership-Followership Paradigm*, states the basic premise behind the leadership-followership state paradigm is that both leadership and followership are states or conditions that can be occupied at various times by persons working in groups, teams, or organizations. A good example of this is when a young military officer first enters a work center. As mentioned before, by law, they are recognized as a leader in a work center. It's not necessarily based on experience. It's based on the fact they are an officer. Many senior officers tell their young officers that if they want to succeed as officers, they must develop a good relationship with their enlisted members. They must seek out that one senior enlisted member and follow their lead. This is an interesting twist because many senior enlisted members have taken young officers under their wings to help develop them as leaders. What this says is that senior leadership recognizes that leadership is not solely based on one's title or rank, but on how much influence a person has over others.

The interaction between officers and enlisted members is similar to that of civilians and military members. Many people don't realize that the senior ranking military member in the Air Force [Air Force Chief of Staff, a 4-star general] reports to the Secretary of the Air Force, a civilian. In the lower echelons, you will find military members leading civilians and civilians leading military members. Misunderstanding often occurs between these two entities because one feels the other cannot relate to their plight. In a case such as this, I have found that communication, respect, and empathy go a long way in building solid relationships between team members.

In a survey that I conducted with past clients, I asked, "What were some of the challenges they faced when following their leaders?" Effective communication and lack of respect were among the top concerns. The same group was asked, "What were some of the challenges they faced when leading others?" Their top responses were lack of initiative and motivation. The next exercise is designed to help you recognize possible hindrances to effective leader-follower relationships, and how you would respond to such issues.

EXERCISE 5

1. How would you respond in a relationship where the leader appears to be incompetent and lacks leadership skills?

_____

_____

_____

2. How would you respond in a relationship where those you lead appear to be incompetent and exhibit poor followership skills?

_____

_____

_____

There are many ways you can approach both scenarios. Whatever you do, I advise you to consider incorporating the following suggestions:

A. Address the behavior and do not attack the person. For example, if the leader is lacking in their ability to make a decision, do not call them a coward. Pull them aside in private and say, "I noticed you were hesitant in making the call in this situation. What prevented you from making this tough decision and how can I help you overcome this in the future?"

B. Listen to what is said and what is not said. A person could say they are not angry or disgruntled but their body language speaks differently.

C. Show some empathy. For example, a leader may say to a follower, "I noticed you didn't meet my suspense date for this particular task. I remember when I was in your shoes, my supervisor asked me to find the answer to a particular problem. Because I didn't have training, I freaked out and dropped the ball." Are you facing a similar situation and if so, how can I help?"

D. Show some respect. Regardless of the role you are serving, everyone deserves respect. Demeaning someone for their inability to do something only creates hostility and hinders communication.

E. Provide training and direction. Everyone does not grasp or learn new concepts in the same manner. It is important to recognize this and provide training in a manner that benefits the trainee.

The aforementioned suggestions are intended to strengthen relationships between leaders and their followers. When both parties set healthy relationships as a top priority, the dividends will be huge. In the next chapter, we will review some of the benefits of the leader-follower partnership.

Chapter 8: Leadership + Followership = Results

*"As a leader, you're probably not doing a good
job unless your employees can do a good impression
of you when you're not around."*

Patrick Lencioni

A healthy leader-follower partnership produces huge
dividends for an organization. Imagine being able to
take a vacation and not worry about a thing because
you know you have capable team members who will
step up and take the lead without any hesitation.
Team members or followers are able to exercise their
leadership skills because you (the formal leader)
have given them ample opportunity to do so. This is
one benefit of having a healthy leader-follower partnership. Below are examples of other benefits:

- Sense of Ownership – When members on the team take ownership of the process, commitment and dedication increases. They don't view coming to work as a job; they view it as an opportunity to do something great. They believe in the vision and the cause and as a result, support it wholeheartedly whether they get a raise or not.
- Personal and Professional Growth – Exemplary leaders and exemplary followers don't settle for the status quo. They live by the motto, "iron sharpens iron." Regardless of the role they are performing at that moment, they recognize that what they are doing is preparing them for another role or greater responsibility. Everything they do will contribute to their character.
- Increased Productivity – Team members perform more effectively and efficiently when there is good morale. Work is no longer work; work is fun! Since everyone on the team is responsible and accountable, they have the latitude to work and play because at the end of the day the work gets done.
- Reduced Tension – Wherever there are people, there will be moments of conflict. Conflict does not have to be bad, but there are times when it becomes quite tense. Nevertheless, exemplary leaders and followers understand the

importance of communication and emotional intelligence. As a result, they can work out differences in a collegial manner.

- Higher Retention Rate - An organization that has healthy team member relationships will notice a high retention rate. People simply do not want to leave a place where they are respected, heard, appreciated, and able to utilize their gifts and talents.

- Appreciation – Appreciation goes both ways in the leader-follower partnership. We often hear that it is important for the leader to express their appreciation to their people. This is true and very much needed, but the same is true of those who follow their leaders. They must let their leader know that they understand and appreciate their efforts. This is just one of those human needs we all have.

The benefits listed are just a few that are produced from healthy leader-follower partnerships. Developing such a partnership takes time but in the long run, it's worth it. There are however, some individuals that may frown upon such relationships because it crosses the line of fraternization between classes of people. For example, in the military, fraternization between officers and enlisted members is prohibited.

The gist of this offense is a violation of the custom of the armed forces against fraternization. However, not all contact or association between officers and enlisted persons is an offense. Whether the contact or association in question is an offense depends on the surrounding circumstances. Factors to be considered include whether the conduct has compromised the chain of command, resulted in the appearance of partiality, or otherwise undermined good order, discipline, authority, or morale. The act and circumstances must be such as to lead a reasonable person experienced in the problems of military leadership to conclude that the good order and discipline of the armed forces has been prejudiced by their tendency to compromise the respect of enlisted persons for the professionalism, integrity, and obligations of an officer (Power, 1995).

In healthy leader-follower partnerships, fraternization does not become a problem because each party understands and respects each other's position. Based on Chaleff's (2003) concepts, his view or fundamental ideas of the leader-follower organization would be applicable in the following situations:

1) By staying aware of our reactions to those we follow, we learn to be more sensitive to our effect on those we lead; and
2) By staying aware of our reactions to those we lead, we learn to be more sensitive in our efforts to support those we follow.

In analyzing Chaleff's view, I can't help but conclude that the ideal team member is one who can identify with both leadership and followership roles and enthusiastically performs either in an exceptional manner. When people on a team are able to set aside their egos and personal agenda, and know their role(s) on the team, then the ability to operate as one team becomes second nature. Operating as one team is critical for team success. The next section of this book will examine how many members can make up a dynamic team.

SECTION C:

OPERATE AS ONE TEAM

Chapter 9: Many Members
Yet One Team

*"It is amazing how much you can accomplish
when it doesn't matter who gets the credit."*

Unknown

How to create effective teams, teamwork, and team building is a challenge in most organizations. Some work environments tend to foster rugged individuals working on personal goals for personal gain. Typically, recognition, reward, and pay systems, single out the achievements of individual employees. Given these factors, is there any reason to wonder why teamwork is an uphill battle in most organizations?

Due to increased competition, limited resources, and the challenge of keeping up with technology, no one becomes successful without a team of competent members. So what defines a team? I would venture to say that a team is a unit comprised of two or more people who work together to achieve a common purpose. I would define a dynamic team as one consisting of individuals who are willing and capable of functioning as a leader and/or a follower to accomplish a common goal.

They are dynamic in nature because roles can be formal or informal. From a formal perspective, a title, along with set responsibilities and authority is assigned to a person and the person keeps this until it's time to change. In an informal setting, another person, even though they don't carry the official title or have the official authority could rise up and assume the leadership role because the situation dictates that a person with certain expertise take the lead. This is often referred to what Ernst Stech coined the leadership-followership state paradigm. Stech (2008) indicated the basic premise behind this paradigm is that both leadership and followership are states or conditions that can be occupied at various times by persons in working groups, teams, or organizations. It is assumed that expertise is diverse and dispensed among the team members. In other words, no one person has all the knowledge or skills required to address an issue. Stech (2008) goes on to say, "Those persons, in positions of authority, must be willing to accept influence from subordinates. They must be willing to assume the condition of followership while a subordinate operates in the state of leadership. The subordinate leads the superior in such a case."

This type of interaction brings about a sense of vulnerability for all parties concerned. The leader must be willing to admit they have areas of ineptness and followers must be willing to admit they need guidance to perform a particular task. In a situation like this, trust becomes a major factor and is required in order for members of the team to display their vulnerabilities.

VITAL PARTS

Every member of the team is a vital component which makes up the whole. Regardless of the role they play, they each must be viewed as a critical piece to the success of the team. To further illustrate this point, the Apostle Paul wrote in the Bible, First Corinthians, chapter 12, verse 12: "The body is a unit, though it is made up of many parts; and though all its parts are many, they form one body." This can be paraphrased in the following manner:

1) The team is a unit, though it is made up of many people; and though the people are many, they form one team.

2) The school is a unit, though it is made up of many departments (support staff, executive staff, English department, music department, technology department); and though the departments are many, they form one school.

3) The United States Armed Forces is a team, though it is made up of many departments (Air Force, Army, Navy, Marines, Coast Guard); and though the departments are many, they form the Armed Forces.
4) The church is a team, though it is made up of many people (teachers, preachers, evangelists, musicians, ushers); and though they are many, they still form one church.

Paul goes on to explain how different each member is to the body, but yet, how important every member is to the body. To further illustrate this point, let's apply this concept to the educational system. A school (the body) is comprised of different departments (English, math, music, PE, technology, teachers, support staff, facilities, etc.) Each department leader <u>follows</u> the direction of the leader (the principal). The principal (the brain) orchestrates the activities of these departments to ensure they are in harmony.

What is equally important is that each department recognizes not only their importance to the team, but the importance of the other departments. There are times when a department head is only concerned about their department. This is not good because failing to empathize with the needs or the demands other departments encounter could affect the overarching goal of student achievement. When the eyes cannot see, the ears and nose increase in their sensitivity so that the body will not run into the wall. Likewise, each department should be willing to help each other and pick up the slack if needed.

This type of camaraderie can be difficult to achieve because many organizations have what they call "friendly competition" among the departments. Because of the competitive nature that resides within some of us, some leaders will use this as a motivator to get individuals to increase productivity and overall profit. For example, they may dangle a carrot in front of a person and say if you out perform your peers you will receive an extra bonus in your paycheck. For those who are competitive in nature, this is a challenge to be met. The rules change from teamwork to "me-work" and this is how conflict begins and wears away at the leader-follower relationship.

Let me share an example of teamwork on a larger scale. Several years ago, my office was hosting its annual leadership conference. It was a time when the Air Force was going through a massive transformation which meant everyone would have to downsize. This was a huge undertaking because as you can imagine, everyone had a valid reason why their office should be exempt from manpower cuts. Their argument was compelling because they laid out their workload for the past several years and the manpower it took to meet their customer's needs. I also did my homework and created a product that compared and contrasted the field offices.

Frustration could be heard in their voices as they presented their case. Some spoke as if they were the only ones in pain. In some cases, the boss and I had to take from one office to boost another office. Those who were receiving additional manpower didn't see a problem with this. However, those who were losing manpower screamed the loudest. When the time came to brief the overall manpower picture, I strategically passed out the chart that was created comparing and contrasting the offices. This was done in an effort to help the field see the bigger picture and to function as a team in providing a viable solution.

What I discovered was that many of the office leaders were focused on their small piece of the world and did not realize how good they had it compared to the other members on the team. What they failed to remember was even though they were geographically separated, they were still members of a larger team. If one part of the team suffers, the other part suffers. People started understanding the magnitude of what was taking place and realized that they too must do their part to ensure manpower requirements were met, as mandated by headquarters. Instead of issuing complaints, they began providing solutions, making concessions, and performing like a dynamic team.

The following exercise provides scenarios for you to examine and discuss how you can foster an environment that exudes teamwork.

EXERCISE 6:

1. In your opinion, what are some of the causes of team dysfunction and what can be done to remedy the problem?

_____

_____

_____

2. You heard the receptionist say, "I'm JUST the receptionist," what would you say to make them feel they are important to the team?

_____

_____

_____

3. You are a manger of a local department store called Banks and you are attending the Banks regional conference for store managers. You hear about the problems other managers are having at their stores. Your store is operating quite well and you recognize you

all are a part of the same team. What would you do to assist the other managers since you are all on the same team?

_____

_____

_____

As you read in the scenarios above, a person's self perception and limited view of the big picture can be a hindrance to effective teamwork. Team members must be aware of their relevance to the team and how they fit into the bigger scheme of things. This can be done by putting everything you have learned about leadership and followership into practice.

Chapter 10: Leadership and Followership: Putting it into Practice

The time has come where many organizations are realizing the benefits of having a flat organizational structure that facilitates open dialogue between its members. According to Stech (2008), in this world of instant communication, technological advances and globalization, the traditional view of the leader, as the hero, the boss, the one who knows all and is all, does not permit an organization to adapt to their ever-changing environments. A paradigm shift recognizes that these roles can be occupied at various times by persons working in groups and team organizations.

Today is the day where organizations must begin to consciously practice exemplary leadership-followership relationships. The success of an organization often lies in the relationships that are established among members of the team. Successful teams realize this and understand that their part in the relationship is crucial. According to Chaleff (2003), "At the heart of all transformation of relationships lies transformation of ourselves, "because this is where we have the most power to create change and the most reluctance to confront the need for it." The following are just a few ways organizations can practice effective leader-follower relationships:

A. **Develop Trust**. Trust is something that comes over time. People will not trust you just because you want them to. You have to earn it. In relationships, people want to know whether or not they can trust you to hold up your end of the bargain. Do you demonstrate competence, integrity, courage, empathy or selflessness? If so, the likelihood of being trusted is great! Another way of looking at trust is being willing to admit that you dropped the ball. This is called humility. No one is perfect and that includes you and me. It is important for both sides (leader and follower) to recognize this fact. When a situation arises where a mistake is made or when a person feels betrayed, instead of saying, "I'll never trust you again" be willing to sit down to discuss what happened, why it happened, and what can be done to prevent it from happening again. After all, we all make mistakes and will continue to make mistakes.

Admitting one's shortcomings and taking steps to correct them can be viewed as creating trust or restoring trust.

B. Respect. "So in everything, do to others what you would have them do to you, for this sums up the Law of the Prophets (NIV: Matthew: 7:12)." This Bible verse captures the essence of respect. I'm often amazed when I hear people complain how their boss mistreats them and they in turn mistreat their subordinates. Everyone deserves respect whether they're the CEO or the janitor. For centuries, there have existed classes of people, the have's and the have not's, the elite and the commoners, the white collar and the blue collar, and the rich and the poor. As a result of these distinctions, disrespect is common which causes increased tension between leadership and their staff. The fact that we are human beings should be the sole factor of why respect is mandatory. Every individual should be recognized for their talent and respected for what they contribute to the organization.

C. Accountability. Often referred to as the father of modern management, Peter Drucker (2001) recognizes the importance of accountability among team members. Individuals, who take responsibility for their contribution in their own work, will, as a rule, demand that their subordinates take responsibility, too.

91

They will tend to ask their subordinates, "What are the contributions for which this organization and I, your supervisor, should hold you accountable? What should we expect of you? What is the best utilization of your knowledge and your ability?

D. **Listen**. Leaders who shut up and listen create an environment where others are willing to listen to them. Encouraging communication at all levels of the organization—and listening to the dialogue that results—raises the bar on individual and group performance (Harari, 2005). It is important that leaders demonstrate they are listening to their followers by openly asking them what they think of a particular situation. Exemplary followers must in turn demonstrate they are listening by responding in a manner that demonstrates critical and analytical thought.

E. **Participate in team-oriented activities**. This is a mechanism to help people develop their interpersonal skills and focus on teamwork.

F. **Provide Feedback**. For many people, receiving feedback can be difficult. I've heard many people say, "Tell it to me straight!" While some can handle this, most people would prefer you tell it straight but with a touch of gentleness. When it comes to providing feedback both leaders and followers would be wise to take the following into consideration:

1. **Self-check**. Do some soul searching before embarking on a mission to tell someone like it is. This can also be painful because the one who is doing the complaining could be the problem. Ask yourself, "What have I done to make the situation better?" If nothing, then do not proceed to providing feedback. Your house must be in order before you try cleaning someone else's.

2. **Respect**. No matter what people may tell you, receiving feedback or criticism is not always easy. In some cases, it flat out hurts! Therefore, when in the position to provide it, do it with the same respect you want shown to you. There is no need to attack the person. Regardless of how bad or unethical this person may appear, deal with the issue or problem along with the reaction it generated. These are facts that the intended receiver must recognize before change in their behavior can occur.

3. **Empathy**. Being able to understand the challenges and stressors both leaders and followers face is critical in developing a healthy relationship. I've heard many people complain about what the leader is or is not doing, and oftentimes, their complaints are based on lack of

empathy, lack of awareness of what the leader is facing, faulty logic, or simply bad information. Followers are not always privy to the competing demands leaders face and the grueling task they encounter in choosing one priority program over another. In addition, leaders must remember their experiences in the follower role and show some empathy when trying to institute policies or changes.

These are just a few concepts about leader-follow relationships that you can put into practice.

Chapter 11: Now What?

"An organization's ability to learn, and translate that learning into action rapidly, is the ultimate competitive advantage."

Jack Welch

I believe that everyone, regardless of their duty, title, or position, can learn to be more effective in their role as a leader and a follower. As you have read, following is something that is required of us depending on the situation we find ourselves placed in. There is nothing wrong with following the lead of another who is acting with integrity.

To maximize the impact of this book, the key is to communicate its ideas to transform your organization into a high impact, dynamic organization that is capable of embracing the challenges of the

21st century; but, you have to have buy-in. Here are several ways to create buy-in:

- Provide a copy of this book to everyone you are trying to influence and share its benefits. Let them know that you have read the book and that it contains ideas and concepts that can improve work relationships and even create a collaborative environment.
- Create a book club where the book can be discussed. Schedule several sessions where individuals can form small groups and delve deeper into specific sections of the book.
- Discuss real world situations that may be similar to the examples in the book. This will make the discussion relevant to the issues or challenges encountered by your team.

Here are just a few of the many questions that could be asked during your discussions?

1. Based on the chapter, *Take* a Good Look at Yourself, what do you see within yourself that could help or hinder team dynamics?
2. What can you, as a leader, do differently to create an environment whereby exemplary followership is the standard?
3. What can you do differently in your role as an exemplary follower, to create an environment of accountability and success?

4. As both a leader and follower, what are your actions portraying to those you lead and to those you follow?

Whoever is facilitating the discussion, make sure everyone is involved. It's best to have small groups when possible this way everyone is afforded the opportunity to contribute to the discussion. In answering the questions, come up with unique ways such as brainstorming, a jeopardy game, individual responses, or round robin exercises whereby every person gives a response, etc.

It is my hope that the concepts in this book will motivate your organization to appreciate the value of leadership and followership and how the two roles connect to form a dynamic team!

JCW Team Consultants, LLC
Motivate...Collaborate...Celebrate!

References

Adair, R. (2008). Developing great leaders, one follower at a time. *The Art of Followership*, 137-155. San Francisco, CA: Jossey-Bass.

Bovee, C.L. & Thill, J. V. (2005). *Excellence in Business Communication.* Upper Saddle River, NJ: Pearson-Prentice Hall.

Chaleff, I. (2003). *The Courageous Follower.* San Francisco, CA: Berrett-Koehler.

Cross, R., & Parker, A. (2004). *The Hidden Power of Social Networks.* Boston, MA: Harvard Business School Publishing.

Dixon, G. (2008). Getting together. *The Art of Followership, 155-176.* San Francisco: Jossey-Bass.

Drucker, P. (2001). *The Essential Drucker.* New York, NY: Harper Collins.

Goleman, D. (1995). *Emotional Intelligence: Why It Can Matter More than IQ.* NewYork, NY: Bantam Dell.

Goleman, D. & Boyatzis, R. (2008). Social intelligence and the biology of leadership. *Harvard Business*

Review. Retrieved from http://hbr.org/2008/09/social-intelligence-and-the-biology-of-leadership/ar/1

Harari, O. (2005). *The Powell Principles: 24 Lessons from Colin Powell Battle-Proven Leader.* Columbus, OH: McGraw Hill Companies.

Kelley, R. (1992). *The Power of Followership: How to Create Leaders People Want to Follow and Followers Who Lead Themselves.* New York, NY: Doubleday.

Maxwell, J. (2001). *Developing the Leader Within You.* Nashville, TN: Thomas Nelson Publishers.

Miller, J. (2001). *QBQ! The Question Behind the Question.* New York, NY: G.P. Putnam's & Sons.

Nolan, J. S. & Harty, H. F. (2001). Followership > leadership. *Education, 104* (3), 311-312.

PBS.org. The American Experience. MacArthur. Retrieved from http://www.pbs.org/wgbh/amex/macarthur/sfeature/officialdocs03.htm

Powell, J. (1995). *Why Am I Afraid to Tell You Who I Am?* Allen, TX: Resource for Christian Living.

Power, R. *Fraternization: When Does Friendship Become a Crime?* Retrieved from http://usmilitary.about.com/od/justicelawlegislation /a/fraternization.-ukn.htm)

Rosenthal, R. & Jacobson, L. (1992). *Pygmalion in the Classroom.* New York, NY: Irvington.

Rost, J.C. (1993). *Leadership for the Twenty-First Century.* Westport, CT.: Praegue.

Scott, J. A. (2005). V-Formation Flight of Birds. Retrieved from http://www.aerospaceweb.org/ question/nature/q0237.shtml

Stech, E. L. (2008). A new leadership-followership paradigm. *The Art of Followership, 41-52.* San Francisco, CA: Jossey-Bass.

Thomas, G. L. *Leadership Lessons From the Life of Thomas Jefferson* - One Leader's Perspective. Retrieved from http://www.leadingtoday.org/ Onmag/2001%20Archives/july01/gt-july01.html

Made in the USA
Charleston, SC
09 February 2012